Uriah Heep

Ham

Betsey Trotwood

Dora

David

Peggotty

Barkis

Miss Murdstone

Traddles

Mr. Dick   Emily   Steerforth

Mr. Peggotty   Agnes   Mr. Micawber

Mrs. Steerforth   Mr. Murdstone   Rosa Dartle

OXFORD ENGLISH PICTURE READERS

Grade Two

DAVID COPPERFIELD

OXFORD ENGLISH PICTURE READERS
COLOUR EDITION

DAVID COPPERFIELD

by **CHARLES DICKENS**
Retold by MARIEL FYEE
Illustrated by JACK TOWNSEND

OXFORD UNIVERSITY PRESS

Oxford University Press, Walton Street, Oxford OX2 6DP

Oxford New York Toronto
Delhi Bombay Calcutta Madras Karachi
Petaling Jaya Singapore Hong Kong Tokyo
Nairobi Dar es Salaam Cape Town
Melbourne Auckland

and associated companies in
Beirut Berlin Ibadan Nicosia

© *Oxford University Press 1974*
First colour edition 1971
Sixteenth impression 1987

OXFORD is a trade mark of Oxford University Press

ISBN 0 19 581125 9

Printed in Hong Kong

Contents

Chapter	Page
1. I AM BORN	7
2. I GO ON HOLIDAY	10
3. MR. PEGGOTTY'S HOUSE	14
4. THE MURDSTONES	18
5. THE SCHOOL	23
6. HOME FOR THE HOLIDAYS	27
7. MY MOTHER DIES	32
8. I GO TO LONDON	36
9. I RUN AWAY	41
10. I STAY WITH MISS BETSEY	44
11. SCHOOL AT CANTERBURY	50
12. I MEET STEERFORTH AGAIN	54
13. I CHOOSE A PROFESSION	62
14. I MEET TOMMY TRADDLES	66
15. I MEET DORA	71
16. I VISIT TRADDLES	76
17. SAD HAPPENINGS AT YARMOUTH	81
18. MR. PEGGOTTY'S SEARCH BEGINS	87
19. I BECOME ENGAGED	90
20. RUIN	93
21. I MARRY DORA	100
22. MARTHA	103
23. I SUFFER LOSS	108
24. THE EMIGRANTS	115
25. I RETURN HOME	117
NOTES	125

At the end of this book you will find notes giving the meaning of some of the words you may not know.

I Am Born

I was born at Blunderstone, in Suffolk, six months after my father's death. The day before my birth, a strange woman came up the garden path. She put her nose against the window, and signed to my mother to open the door.

'You are Mrs. David Copperfield,' she said.

'Yes,' said my mother.

'I am Miss Betsey Trotwood,' said the visitor. 'I expect you have heard of me.'

My mother had never seen Miss Betsey before. She was my father's aunt, and she had quarrelled with him when he married. Her home was at Dover.

Mother took her into the parlour. As they sat by the fire, Mother felt so ill and unhappy she began to cry.

'Come, come, you must not do that,' said Miss Betsey, touching my mother's beautiful hair. 'When your baby is born, I am going to be her friend. You must call her Betsey Trotwood Copperfield.'

'Perhaps the baby will be a boy,' said my mother.

'I am sure it will be a girl,' said Miss Betsey firmly.

A few hours later, when the doctor told her the baby had arrived safely and was a boy, my aunt was very angry.

She took her bonnet by the strings and hit the doctor's head with it. Then she put the bonnet on her head, walked out of the house, and never came back.

9

CHAPTER 2

I go on Holiday

I was called David Copperfield, after my father.
My mother and I lived in Rookery Cottage, along
with our servant, Peggotty.

Peggotty was our friend as well as our servant.
When we were alone, she sat with us in the parlour
in the evening. She always had her workbox beside
her. It had a picture of St. Paul's Cathedral on the
lid.

Mother, Peggotty, and I were very happy together, until one day my mother met Mr. Murdstone.

Mr. Murdstone was tall, dark, and handsome, and had black whiskers. He often came to the house to see my mother. I did not like him, nor did Peggotty.

One day Peggotty said to me, 'Would you like to come with me to Yarmouth to spend a fortnight with my brother? You would see the sea and boats.'

'I'd like that, Peggotty, but what would my mother do? She cannot live alone,' I replied.

'Oh, I think she will let you come with me. She'll go away herself, and stay with friends.'

A few days later, Mother watched us climb on to the carrier's cart which was to take us to Yarmouth. There were tears in her eyes, and she kissed me many times before the cart moved off.

As we drove away, Mr. Murdstone came up to her, and I could see that he was cross when he saw her tears.

'What business is it of Mr. Murdstone's?' I thought angrily. I could see from Peggotty's face that she was angry with him too.

The carrier's horse went very slowly, and it took
us a long time to get to Yarmouth. I was glad when
at last we arrived.

Yarmouth smelt of fish and tar. As we drove in,
Peggotty cried out:

'Oh, look! There's my nephew, Ham, waiting for
us.'

Ham was a huge, strong fellow, with light curly
hair, and a simple face. He was dressed in a canvas
jacket and stiff trousers.

13

CHAPTER 3

Mr. Peggotty's House

Ham carried me on his back through the town, towards the sea.

'Yon's our house, Master Davy,' he said when we reached a long flat stretch of sand.

All I could see was an old black boat, high and dry on the sand.

'That's not it?' I asked. 'That ship-looking thing?'

'That's it, Mas'er Davy,' he replied.

I was delighted with the idea of living in a boat for a house.

The house was beautifully clean inside. Peggotty opened a little door at one end of the boat and showed me my bedroom. It was the neatest room, with a little window, a little looking-glass, and a little bed.

A woman in a white apron, and a beautiful little girl called Emily, welcomed us. I tried to kiss Emily, but she ran away.

Soon Mr. Peggotty, Peggotty's brother, came home. He was a large, hairy man with a good-natured face.

After tea, when the door was shut, everything was snug inside the boat. Little Emily sat beside me on a box by the fire.

I thought the woman in the apron was Mr. Peggotty's wife, and that Ham and Emily were their children. But Mr. Peggotty told me he was not married.

'My brother, Joe, was Ham's father,' he said, 'and he was drowned.'

'And little Emily?' I asked.

'My brother-in-law, Tom, was her father,' Mr. Peggotty answered, 'and he was drowned.'

'And who is that?' I asked pointing to the woman who was knitting.

'That is Mrs. Gummidge.'

Peggotty told me afterwards that Mrs. Gummidge's husband had shared Mr. Peggotty's boat. When he died, the good-hearted Mr. Peggotty took Mrs. Gummidge to his home and looked after her.

Mrs. Gummidge was always being miserable. If anything went wrong she would cry, 'I'm a lone lorn creature, and everything goes contrary with me.'

Instead of being angry with her, Mr. Peggotty would remember she had lost her husband and he would feel sorry for her.

'She's been thinking of the old 'un,' he would say.

CHAPTER 4

The Murdstones

Soon it was time for Peggotty and me to go home. I hated leaving little Emily, but I looked forward to seeing my mother again.

The moment we reached the door of the Rookery I knew something was wrong. Instead of my mother, a strange maid met us.

'Peggotty, where's my mother? She's not dead?'

'No,' said Peggotty, breathing hard. 'You've got a new father. Come and see him.'

Peggotty took me to the parlour, and there I saw my mother sitting on one side of the fire and Mr. Murdstone on the other.

My mother rose quickly to kiss me, but she looked a little afraid.

'Clara, don't fuss,' said Mr. Murdstone. He shook my hand, and mother kissed me; but I could not look at her.

As soon as I could, I crept upstairs. My bedroom was changed—everything was changed for me.

Mr. Murdstone's sister came to stay with us. She was very hard and harsh, and she did not like boys.

Miss Murdstone took charge of the household. My mother was no longer mistress in her own house. She had to do exactly as she was told by Mr. and Miss Murdstone. Mr. Murdstone said he would beat me if I did not do just what he told me.

Mr. and Miss Murdstone used to sit in the room while I repeated my lessons. When I forgot them, Mr. Murdstone beat me with a cane.

One day he took me to my room to beat me. I caught his hand in my mouth and bit his finger. After that he beat me as if he would have beaten me to death.

He shut me in my room for five days, and I saw no one but Miss Murdstone. But Peggotty came and talked to me through the keyhole. She told me I was to go to school in London the next day.

Next day, I cried when my mother put me on the carrier's cart and kissed me good-bye.

We had not gone far when Peggotty ran into the road and stopped the cart. She gave me a hug, a parcel of cakes, and some money. Then she ran away.

I gave Mr. Barkis, the carrier, a cake.

'Did she make them?' he asked.

'Yes, Peggotty does all our cooking,' I replied.

'Then if you write to her, will you please remember to say, "Barkis is willing"? Yes, that's the message. "Barkis is willing."'

CHAPTER 5

The School

Salem House, the school I was sent to, was on holi-day when I arrived, but Mr. Creakle, the head-master, had left a notice to be pinned on my back. It said, 'TAKE CARE OF HIM. HE BITES.'

No one knows what I suffered from that notice. I could never forget it, and felt that someone was always reading it.

The first boy to see it was Tommy Traddles.

'Look, here's a game,' he cried, and he showed the notice to each boy as he arrived.

I was shown to J. Steerforth, a tall handsome boy, who appeared to be head of the school. He asked me questions about my punishment, and then said, 'It's a jolly shame'.

He became my friend for life after that. He took charge of the money Peggotty had given me and spent it on food, which he divided out among the boys.

'I'll take care of you, young Copperfield,' said Steerforth.

He did, and I was grateful to him.

Steerforth could not protect me from Mr. Creakle, the headmaster. He was a very cruel man, who beat all the boys with a cane—all but Steerforth. Traddles suffered terribly from his punishments. He was caned every day, but he managed to keep cheerful in spite of that. When Mr. Creakle found that the cardboard on my back kept him from cutting me with his cane, he had the notice removed.

At nights, when we went to bed, Steerforth used to make me tell him stories from all the books I had read. In return, he helped me with my sums.

25

One day, Mr. Peggotty and Ham came to visit me at school.

'How is little Emily?' I asked.

'She is growing into a woman,' said Mr. Peggotty. 'She is so pretty and clever.'

Steerforth happened to pass through the hall while I was speaking to them, and I introduced them to him.

'Tell them at home that Mr. Steerforth is very kind to me,' I said. 'I don't know what I'd do without him.'

Steerforth talked to the two fishermen. Mr. Peggotty invited him to come with me to visit them in Yarmouth, any time he pleased.

CHAPTER 6

Home for Holidays

After six months, I went home in the carrier's cart for the holidays.

'I gave Peggotty your message, Mr. Barkis,' I said.

'Nothing came of it. No answer,' said Mr. Barkis gruffly. 'When a man says he's willing, he expects an answer.'

'Would you like me to tell her?' I asked.

'You might tell her, if you would, that Barkis is waiting for an answer.'

Mr. Barkis put my box at the gate and left me.

I walked up the path, glancing at the windows to see if anyone was looking for me. I went into the hall, and heard my mother singing in a low voice, as she used to sing to me when I was a baby.

I went softly into the room, and found her sitting by the fire with a tiny baby in her arms.

When I spoke to her, my mother jumped to her feet. She kissed me, then she put the baby's hand to my lips.

'He is your brother,' she said.

Peggotty came running in, and kissed and hugged me. Mr. and Miss Murdstone had gone to visit friends, and we three were alone for supper. We had our meal together as we used to do.

When I told Peggotty about Mr. Barkis, she threw her apron over her face, and laughed.

'What's the matter, Peggotty?' asked my mother.

'He wants to marry me,' laughed Peggotty.

Though my mother laughed with Peggotty, I saw she looked afraid.

Mother was very pretty still, but she looked pale and delicate.

'Don't leave me, Peggotty,' she said. 'Stay with me. It will not be for long, perhaps.'

'Me leave you?' cried Peggotty. 'Not for all the world.'

We sat round the fire talking. Peggotty was mending a stocking. I told them what a hard man Mr. Creakle was, and how much I liked Steerforth.

'I wonder what has happened to Davy's great aunt, Miss Betsey Trotwood,' Peggotty said suddenly.

'Don't talk of such uncomfortable things,' said my mother. 'Miss Betsey is shut up in her cottage by the sea. She is not likely ever to trouble us again.'

I was at home for a month, and the holidays dragged past. Mr. and Miss Murdstone made me feel I was not wanted, yet they would not allow me to sit in my own room, or with Peggotty in the kitchen. I had to sit for hours in the parlour, without moving a hand or foot lest I should disturb them.

I was not sorry to go back to school on Mr. Barkis's cart. As I left home I looked back and saw my mother standing alone at the garden gate, holding up the baby for me to see. That is how I remember her now.

CHAPTER 7

My Mother Dies

One day in March, Mr. Creakle sent for me to go to his study. Mrs. Creakle was there with a letter in her hand. She led me to a couch, and told me my mother was dead.

I cried myself to sleep that night. The next day I went home to my mother's funeral. My baby brother died a few hours after my mother, and they were buried together. I shall never forget how sad and lonely I felt.

Peggotty was a great comfort to me, but Mr. and Miss Murdstone took no notice of me, either that day or in the days that followed. They seemed to hate the sight of me.

I asked if I was to go back to school.

'No,' they replied, but they did not say what was to happen to me.

I spent the time with Peggotty in the kitchen, and kept out of the way of Mr. and Miss Murdstone.

After the funeral, Miss Murdstone told Peggotty she must find another job. Peggotty looked for work in Blunderstone, so that she would be near me, but she could not find any.

'I shall go to Yarmouth for a fortnight, and take you with me,' said Peggotty.

Mr. Barkis called for us in his cart, and on the journey he tried to make friends with Peggotty. He sat so close to her that we were all crowded to one side of the cart.

When we reached Yarmouth, Peggotty said to me, 'Davy, what would you think if I were to marry Barkis?'

'It would be a very good thing,' I said. 'You could come in the cart to see me often.'

34

Two weeks later, Peggotty and Barkis were married, and went to live in his neat little cottage. There was a small room in the roof which Peggotty said was for me.

'I shall keep it every day, as I used to keep your old little room, my darling,' she said.

I shall never forget how unhappy I was when Barkis and Peggotty took me back to Blunderstone. Day after day, Mr. and Miss Murdstone took no notice of me. At last, a friend of Mr. Murdstone's suggested I should go and work in London.

CHAPTER 8

I go to London

I was ten years old when I was sent to London to
wash bottles in a wine merchant's business. It was
an old building beside the river. I worked beside
four other boys in a damp cellar, for six shillings a
week. The boys were rough and the work was hard.
I was very unhappy.

Mr Murdstone arranged that I should lodge with
a Mr. and Mrs. Micawber and their children, in a
shabby house in Windsor Terrace. Mr. Micawber
was a commercial traveller who owed money to all
who would give him credit. From morning to night,
tradesmen came to the house demanding that their
accounts should be paid.

Mr. Micawber was a fat middle-aged man, with a large face and a shiny bald head. His clothes were old and worn, but he wore them with a great air, and he spoke in a very grand way. Mrs. Micawber was thin and pale.

When they were very short of money, Mrs. Micawber would often ask me to sell pieces of furniture and books for her. She bought food with the money I got for them, and cooked us all a good supper.

One day Mr. Micawber was sent to prison because he could not pay his debts. I thought his heart would break, and that mine would break too. Mrs. Micawber and the children went to live in the prison with him. I found a room not far away, and visited them often.

When Mr. Micawber came out of prison, he decided to leave London with his family, and seek his fortune in Plymouth. We all shed tears when I waved good-bye to them, as they set off on the Plymouth coach.

Mr. and Mrs. Micawber were my only friends, and I was very lonely without them. I was so unhappy at the warehouse that I decided to run away. I would go and look for my aunt, Betsey Trotwood.

I wrote to ask Peggotty to send me a little money, and Miss Betsey's address. Peggotty replied at once. She sent me ten shillings, and told me all she knew of my aunt was that she lived in Dover.

CHAPTER 9

I Run Away

After work on Saturday I hurried to my lodgings to collect my belongings. My box was so large and heavy, I could not carry it. On the way I spoke to a tall young man with a donkey cart, and asked him if he would take my box to the Dover coach office for sixpence.

He agreed, and put the box on the cart, but he drove off at such a speed, that I had to run to keep up with him.

At the coach station, I was so excited and tired, that I dropped Peggotty's money. The young man grabbed it, and would not give it back to me.

He jumped into the cart, sat on my box, and drove away faster than ever. I ran after him through the streets, bumping into people, falling in the mud, trying to keep up with him. The young man drove off with my box and my money, and I never saw him again.

I started to walk to Dover. I had only three-halfpence in my pocket, so I sold my waistcoat for ninepence. I slept the night under a haystack, and the next day I plodded on.

After walking for six days I reached Dover. I had sold my jacket as well as my waistcoat, and now I was dusty, hungry, and half-naked.

I kept asking people if they knew where Miss Betsey Trotwood lived. I went into a shop and asked the shopman. He was serving a young woman. She turned quickly.

'Miss Trotwood? That's my mistress. What do you want with her, boy?' she asked.

'I want to speak to her, please.'

The maid led me to a neat little cottage with a garden full of flowers.

'This is Miss Trotwood's,' she said, leaving me at the garden gate. A pleasant faced man nodded and laughed at me from a top window.

The house was so neat, and I was so ragged, I almost ran away in fright. Then a lady, wearing a handkerchief over her cap, came out of the house. I knew it was Miss Betsey.

'Go away,' she cried. 'No boys here.'

CHAPTER 10

I Stay with Miss Betsey

Miss Betsey went to the corner of the garden and began digging. I stood beside her, and touched her arm.

'If you please, Aunt,' I said. 'I am your nephew. I am David Copperfield, of Blunderstone.' She started, dropped her spade, and sat down on the garden path.

'Eh?' she said.

'You came to Blunderstone the night I was born, and saw my dear mother. I have been very unhappy since she died.'

I began to cry, and Miss Betsey jumped up.

44

My aunt took me into the house and gave me something to drink. She made me lie on the couch, and put a shawl under my head. Then she told the maid to fetch Mr. Dick.

When he came into the room, I saw he was the man who had nodded to me from the window.

'Mr. Dick, this is my nephew's son. He has run away. What shall I do with him?'

'I should wash him,' he replied.

'Mr. Dick sets us all right,' said Miss Betsey 'Janet, heat the bath.'

45

My aunt was tall, with a strong face, and quick bright eyes. Her hair was grey and straight, and she wore neat plain clothes.

In front of her house there was a smooth patch of grass. Often people passed the house riding donkeys, and if they allowed the donkeys to stray on to the grass, my aunt was furious.

'Janet!' she'd cry. 'Donkeys!'

The two women would then rush out and chase away the donkeys and their riders, sometimes with sticks, or jugs of water.

Mr. Dick had grey hair and a round red face. I thought he was a little mad, but my aunt said he certainly was not. It was because his relations thought him mad that she had brought him to live with her, ten years before.

Mr. Dick spent his days writing a book, and flying a huge kite.

'He is the most friendly creature,' said my aunt, 'and gives such good advice. What would you do with David's son, Mr. Dick?'

'Put him to bed,' said Mr. Dick.

I had not been long with my aunt when she wrote to Mr. Murdstone. He replied that he would come and see her next day. Late in the afternoon my aunt jumped up with her cry of, 'Donkeys!', and shook her fist through the window. I saw Miss Murdstone sitting on a donkey, on the patch of grass.

'It's Miss Murdstone,' I told her.

'I don't care who it is. Janet, turn them off.'

Mr. Murdstone appeared behind his sister, and joined in the battle.

That afternoon, my aunt told Mr. Murdstone exactly what she thought of him for ill-treating my mother and me.

'I am here to take David back,' said he. 'If you keep him from coming with us now, you must keep him for ever.'

'Are you ready to go, David?' asked my aunt.

I begged her not to let me go. I prayed her to befriend me, for my father's sake.

'Mr. Dick, what shall I do with this child?' she asked.

'Have him measured at once for a suit of clothes,' he answered.

'Mr. Dick, give me your hand,' cried my aunt. 'You always give such good advice.'

Then she turned to the Murdstones.

'Good day, and good-bye,' she said to them. 'If I see you ride a donkey over my grass again, I'll knock your bonnet off and tread on it.'

CHAPTER 11

School at Canterbury

Miss Betsey sent me to a school in Canterbury, kept by Dr. Strong. How different it was from Salem House, Mr. Creakle's school.

Dr. Strong was good and kind, and he was greatly loved by everybody. There was not room for me to live in school, and my aunt's lawyer, Mr. Wickfield, invited me to stay with him and his daughter, Agnes.

Agnes was a sweet gentle girl of about my own age. Her mother was dead, and she looked after her father's house. I was very happy with the Wickfields.

Mr. Wickfield had a clerk, called Uriah Heep. I disliked him the first time I saw him. He had short red hair, with pale eyebrows and eyelashes, and he used to keep rubbing his damp hands together.

'I suppose you are going to be a great lawyer,' I said to Uriah, one day in the office.

'Oh no,' he replied. 'I'm a very 'umble person. My mother is also a very 'umble person. We live in an 'umble house, Master Copperfield, but we have much to be thankful for.'

One day I was invited to have tea with Uriah
Heep and his mother. Mrs. Heep looked like Uriah,
only she was smaller.

'My Uriah has looked forward to this for a long
while,' she said. ' 'Umble we are, 'umble we have
been, 'umble we ever shall be.'

'I am sure you have no need to be so,' I said,
'unless you like.'

Uriah and Mrs. Heep made me talk far too much
about my aunt, my mother and father, my step-
father, Mr. Wickfield and Agnes. They made me
tell them things I had no business to tell.

The door opened from their sitting-room right on to the street. A man, who was passing the house, looked in at the open door. He turned back and came into the house.

'Copperfield! Is it possible?' he cried.

It was Mr. Micawber. We were delighted to see one another. I introduced him to Uriah and his mother.

Mr. Micawber told me he and his wife had come to Canterbury, in the hope that something would turn up. As usual, they were very short of money.

53

CHAPTER 12

I Meet Steerforth Again

The time came for me to leave school. I was seventeen, and felt grown up.

'What would you like to be?' my aunt kept asking me.

I had no idea. All I wanted was to earn my own living, so that I should not be a burden to her.

'I tell you what,' she said to me one morning. 'Go and have a holiday, and think it over.'

And so, with a purse of money and my luggage, I set off alone.

First I went to Canterbury, to say good-bye to Mr. Wickfield and Agnes.

Agnes had grown up. She was gentle and beautiful, but she looked worried.

'Do you see any change in father, David?' she asked.

'His hand shakes, and his voice is not clear,' I said.

'Yes,' said Agnes, 'and when he is at his worst, Uriah worries him with business.'

When I left Canterbury, I went to an hotel at Charing Cross, in London.

55

I was sitting in the coffee room when a handsome young man came into the hotel. As I passed him on my way to my bedroom, I knew who he was, though he did not know me.

'Steerforth!' I said, 'won't you speak to me?'

'It's little Copperfield!' he cried, shaking hands.

We had not met since our schooldays at Salem House. He was on his way to visit his mother at Highgate, and he begged me to go with him, and stay for a few days.

Steerforth's mother lived in a large house with her companion, Rosa Dartle. She was very proud of her son, and talked to me for hours about him.

Miss Dartle was thin, and dark, and not very pretty. She kept asking questions.

'I only ask for information,' she would say.

She had a scar on her lip. When I asked Steerforth about it, he replied sadly:

'I did that when I was young. She angered me, and I threw a hammer at her.'

I was sorry I had spoken about it.

I stayed at Highgate for a week, then I persuaded Steerforth to come with me to Yarmouth for a holiday.

When we arrived we took our luggage to the inn, before I went to visit Peggotty.

'Is Mr. Barkis at home ma'am,' I asked in a gruff voice, when she opened the door. It was seven years since we had met, and she did not know me.

'He's at home, sir, but he's ill.'

'I want to ask about the Rookery.' I said.

Peggotty stepped back with surprise.

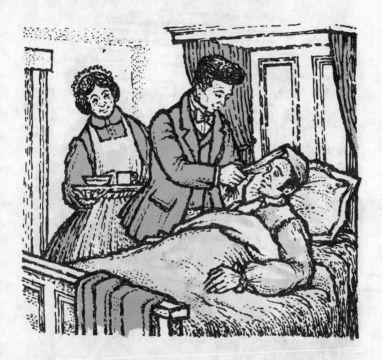

'Peggotty!' I cried to her.

'My darling boy!' she cried.

She opened her arms and hugged me. How we laughed and cried together. Presently she said, 'Will you come up and see Barkis?'

Barkis was in bed. He was too rheumatic for me to shake hands with him, but he begged me to shake the tassel on his nightcap. We talked of old times.

Soon Steerforth arrived. He was so pleasant to Barkis and Peggotty that they loved him at once.

That evening, I took Steerforth to visit Mr. Peggotty. When we opened the door of the boat, Mr. Peggotty was standing with a glad smile on his face. Ham and Emily were standing before him, hand in hand, and Mrs. Gummidge, usually so sad, was in a corner clapping her hands like a mad woman.

When they saw us, they gave us a great welcome.

'Little Emily is to marry Ham,' cried Mr. Peggotty.

'I'd lay down my life for her, Master Davy,' said Ham.

Emily was shy, but Steerforth spoke in such an easy way, that soon we were all talking happily together.

We left the house about midnight.

'Emily is a little beauty,' said Steerforth, 'but isn't Ham rather a rough fellow for her?'

I was shocked by this cold remark from Steerforth, who had been so pleasant to them all. But when I looked at him, his eyes were laughing, and I thought he did not mean to be unkind.

Steerforth often went sailing with the fishermen. Before we left Yarmouth he told me he had bought a boat.

'I'll call her the *Little Em'ly*,' he said, 'and Mr. Peggotty will be master of her while I am away.'

We made many friends among the fishermen, and they were sorry when we left Yarmouth in the coach.

CHAPTER 13

I Choose a Profession

I met my aunt at Lincoln's Inn Fields, in London.

'How would you like to become a proctor—a lawyer?' she asked.

'I should like it very much,' I replied, 'but won't that cost a lot of money?'

'A thousand pounds,' said Miss Betsey, 'but I want to make you a good, sensible, happy man.'

We went to the office of Messrs. Spenlow and Jorkins, lawyers in the City. Mr. Spenlow agreed to allow me to become an apprentice in the firm, for the sum of a thousand pounds.

Then my aunt took me to look for rooms in
Buckingham Street, where there was a small flat to
let. After ringing the bell several times, Mrs. Crupp,
the fat landlady, opened the door. She took us to the
top of the house and showed us a sitting-room, a
bedroom, and a small dark pantry. The furniture
was faded, but I was delighted with the place, and
at once rented it.

When all the arrangements were made, my aunt
went back to Dover.

At first, I liked being free to go in and out of my rooms as I liked. After a day or two, however, I began to feel lonely, especially in the evening.

Steerforth had not come to see me. When at last he walked in one morning at breakfast, I was delighted. I made him promise to bring two of his friends to have dinner with me one evening.

I ordered extra food and wine, and we had a very merry party.

Unfortunately, I kept passing the wine round until I had drunk too much. Someone suggested going to the theatre. We went, but the wine had made me so stupid, I could not understand the play.

In the theatre, I found myself face to face with Agnes Wickfield. She drew back when she saw me. When I tried to talk to her, she begged, 'David, for my sake, go away. Ask your friends to take you home.'

The next thing I knew was that I was in my own bed. It was morning when I wakened.

CHAPTER 14

I Meet Tommy Traddles

The day after the party I felt ill and ashamed of myself. How could I find Agnes, to tell her I was sorry for my bad behaviour at the theatre?

As I was leaving my lodgings, I was handed a letter. It was from Agnes.

'I am staying with a business friend of Papa's, Mr. Waterbrook, in Ely Place, Holborn,' she wrote. 'Will you come and see me today?'

I went to Holborn at four o'clock, and with tears in my eyes, I asked Agnes to forgive me.

'You are my good angel, Agnes,' I said.

'Then I should warn you against your bad angel,' she said.

'Do you mean Steerforth?'

'I do.' she replied.

'You wrong him, Agnes. He is my good friend.'

'He is a dangerous friend,' said Agnes.

'Do not judge him by what you saw of me the other night,' I begged. I told her how Steerforth had looked after me, when I could not look after myself.

Agnes told me she had bad news. Uriah Heep was going to become a partner in her father's business, instead of being only a clerk.

'You must not allow that mean fellow, Uriah, to become a partner,' I cried.

'I can't stop him,' said Agnes. 'Father has agreed to the plan, because he is afraid of him. Uriah is in London now, David. If you meet him, be nice to him for my sake.'

Before I could reply, Mrs. Waterbrook came into the room, and asked me to dine with them next day. I accepted her invitation, and then went home.

When I arrived at the Waterbrooks' house the following day, I found Uriah Heep already there. He was in a black suit, and as humble as ever. He stood close by Agnes and me, so that he could hear every word we said.

Among the guests was a Mr. Traddles. I looked at the young man to see if he was the Tommy Traddles I had known at Salem House. He was, and we were delighted to meet again.

Tommy was studying law. He was greatly interested to hear that I had met Steerforth.

DAVID COPPERFIELD

Tommy had to leave the party early, but we exchanged addresses and promised to meet again some other time.

Uriah and I left the house together. I asked him to come home with me for coffee. He told me he had been so useful to Mr. Wickfield that he had been asked to become a partner in his business.

Then he talked of his love for Agnes till I could have struck him, I hated him so much. When he left, I opened all the windows to clear the air of him.

CHAPTER 15

I Meet Dora

When I had been in the office of Spenlow and
Jorkins for several weeks, Mr. Spenlow invited me
to his home in Norwood for a week-end.

I knew his wife was dead, and that he had a
daughter newly home from school in Paris. Mr.
Spenlow drove me to Norwood in his carriage. He
had a fine house, and a beautiful garden.

71

'Mr. Copperfield, this is my daughter, Dora, and her companion,' he said, when we arrived.

'Dora! What a lovely name,' I thought.

She was a small dainty creature. I loved her from the moment I saw her.

'I have seen Mr. Copperfield before,' said a voice I remembered well.

The voice was not Dora's. It was the companion who spoke—Miss Murdstone! My thoughts were too much with Dora to feel surprised.

'How do you do, Miss Murdstone,' I said.

'I am glad to find that you and Miss Murdstone know each other,' said Mr. Spenlow.

'I knew Mr. Copperfield when he was young,' said Miss Murdstone.

After dinner, Miss Murdstone took me aside.

'David Copperfield,' she said, 'I know what I think of you, and doubtless you have your opinion of me, but while we are here, we need not show our feelings. Do you agree?'

'Miss Murdstone,' I answered, 'I shall always think you and Mr. Murdstone treated my mother and me very cruelly, but I agree to keep quiet about what happened in the past.'

For the rest of the evening I gazed at Dora as she played and sang to us. I was madly in love with her. She smiled and gave me her hand when she bade me good night, and I could not sleep for thinking of her.

Next morning, I got up early and went into the garden. Dora's little dog, Jip, was there. Everything about Dora thrilled me. I even loved Jip, but when I spoke to him, he showed all his teeth, and snarled Then I saw Dora, with a straw hat trimmed with blue ribbons on her fair curls.

We talked for a little, then she said, 'You don't know Miss Murdstone well, do you?'

'No, I don't.' I replied.

'She is a tiresome person,' said Dora. 'We don't like her, do we, Jip?'

When I went back to town, I could think of nothing but Dora. I bought three fancy waistcoats. I wore shoes that were too small for me, and walked miles through the streets, because I hoped to see her again.

I went off my food. Even Mrs. Crump, my landlady, knew I was in love, though I told her nothing about Dora.

'Mr. Copperfield,' she said, 'I'm a mother myself, and my advice to you is to cheer up and know your own value.'

CHAPTER 16

I Visit Traddles

I went to visit Traddles, and he gave me a great welcome. He rented a room on the top floor of an untidy house.

He told me about his struggle to become a lawyer. He had become engaged to a curate's daughter in Devonshire.

'She's the dearest girl,' he said, 'but we shall not have money to marry for a long time. I board with the people downstairs. Both Mr. and Mrs. Micawber are good company.'

'Mr. and Mrs. Micawber!' I repeated, 'I know them well.'

At that moment Mr. Micawber knocked at the door, and Traddles invited him to come in.

'How do you do, Mr. Micawber,' I said.

'Very well, I thank you sir,' he replied politely.

It was so long since we had met that he did not know me. I smiled at him, which made him look at me more closely.

'Is it possible?' he cried. 'Is it really Copperfield, the friend of my youth?'

He took both my hands and shook them. Mrs. Micawber came into the room, and almost fainted when they told her who I was. She, too, was delighted to see me.

Before leaving, I asked Traddles and the Micaw-
bers to come one day and have dinner with me.

They accepted my invitation.

During the party Steerforth's manservant arrived,
asking for him.

'I have not seen him for a long time,' I said.

That evening, when my guests left, Steerforth
himself arrived. He said he had come from Yarmouth, and he brought me a letter from Peggotty
telling me that Barkis was very ill.

'I think I shall go to Yarmouth to visit my old nurse,' I said.

'Before you go, come with me to Highgate for a night to visit my mother,' said Steerforth. 'If you don't, who knows when we shall meet again.'

I agreed to go with him next day.

Mrs. Steerforth and Rosa Dartle were pleased to see me. Rosa Dartle took me aside, and asked me why Steerforth had been so long away from home.

'What is he doing?' she asked.

'I don't know what you mean,' I replied.

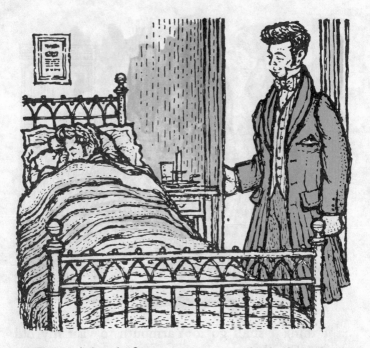

That night, before we went to bed, Steerforth
said to me:

'David, if anything should ever come between us,
you must think of me at my best.'

'You have no best to me, Steerforth,' I said, 'and
no worst. You are always my friend.'

Next morning, before I left for Yarmouth, I looked into Steerforth's room. He was fast asleep, lying
easily with his head upon his arm, as I had often
seen him lie at school.

CHAPTER 17

Sad Happenings at Yarmouth

I reached Peggotty's cottage about ten o'clock at night. Mr. Peggotty answered my knock, and took me into the kitchen. Ham and Emily were there, and we all talked in whispers—all but Emily who clung to her uncle, and did not say a word.

There was something strange about Emily. She would not leave her uncle to go with Ham, who had come to take her home.

Barkis was dying. Peggotty came downstairs from his room, and begged me to come and see him.

'Barkis, my dear,' said Peggotty, 'here's Master David, who brought us together. You sent a message by him—remember? Won't you speak to him, Barkis?'

Barkis tried to stretch out his arm. He smiled, and said to me quite clearly, 'Barkis is willing'. Then he died.

Peggotty begged me to stay at Yarmouth till after the funeral. I was able to help her by taking charge of Barkis's will. He left £3,000. He left £1,000 to Mr. Peggotty and the rest to Peggotty, which kept her in comfort.

After the funeral, I went to spend the evening at the boat house. It looked very comfortable indeed. Mr. Peggotty smoked his pipe, Peggotty was in her old place with her sewing. Mrs. Gummidge was in her corner, grumbling as usual.

We sat waiting for Ham to bring Emily home from her work as a dressmaker. Mr. Peggotty rose, and put a lighted candle in the window.

'That's for our little Em'ly,' he laughed. 'Even when she's married, I know I'll still put the candle there. Listen, there she is.'

It was not Emily. It was only Ham, with a large sou'wester over his face.

'Where's Emily?' said Mr. Peggotty, bending down to mend the fire.

'Master Davy, will you come out a minute?' said Ham.

As I went out, I saw he was deadly pale. He pushed me into the open air and shut the door.

'Ham, what's the matter?' I asked.

'Master Davy——' Ham broke down and cried. 'Emily has gone. She's run away. How shall I tell him, Master Davy?'

Mr. Peggotty rushed out of the house, followed by Peggotty and Mrs. Gummidge. I shall never forget the look on his face.

Ham handed me a letter to read aloud. It was from Emily.

'When you get this,' she wrote, 'I shall be gone. I will never come back, unless he marries me. Love some good girl who will be true to you, and tell Uncle I've never loved him so much as I do now.'

'Who is the man?' asked Mr. Peggotty.

'Go away, Master Davy, while I tell him,' said Ham.

'Don't tell me his name is Steerforth,' gasped Mr. Peggotty.

'Aye, it's Steerforth,' said Ham, 'and he's a black-hearted villain! He and his servant have been hiding about here for a week or two. He is the man!'

Mr. Peggotty put on his coat.

'Where are you going?' asked Ham.

'I am going to look for Emily,' he replied. 'But I'm going first to smash that boat. If I had known what Steerforth was going to do, I'd have drowned him, and thought it right. I'm going to look for my niece, and bring her back.'

'No, no,' said Mrs. Gummidge, 'don't go as you are. Wait till you are not so angry.'

Mr. Peggotty became quiet, and soon I heard him crying.

CHAPTER 18

Mr. Peggotty's Search Begins

The next day, Mr. Peggotty and Peggotty went with me to London. I found lodgings for them in a house not far from my own.

Mr. Peggotty wanted to see Mrs. Steerforth, and I took him to the house in Highgate.

Mrs. Steerforth had already heard from her son, and she looked pale and worried.

'I am sorry for what has happened,' she said, 'but what can I do?'

'Will your son marry Emily?' asked Mr. Peggotty.

'Never,' she replied. 'She would not make a suitable wife for him. His career would be ruined.'

'I came here with no hope, and I take away no hope,' said Mr. Peggotty sadly.

As we left the house, Rosa Dartle spoke to me. Her face was dark with anger.

'What do you mean, bringing that fellow here?' she said.

'He has suffered greatly, Miss Dartle,' I replied, 'though you may not know it.'

'I know James Steerforth is false and wicked,' she said. 'But what do I care about that man and his niece? She should be slapped and put in the streets to starve. I hate her.'

88

Without a word Mr. Peggotty left the house. I followed him, and asked him where he was going.

'I am going, sir, to seek my niece,' he replied.

We had supper with Peggotty, then Mr. Peggotty got out his oilskin bag, and his stout stick.

'If anything should happen to me,' he said, 'tell Emily my last words were, "My unchanged love is with my darling child, and I forgive her."'

Peggotty and I went with him to the door, and watched him turn the corner and go out of sight.

CHAPTER 19

I Become Engaged

All this time I had been loving Dora more than
ever, and when Mr. Spenlow invited me to a picnic
party, I was greatly delighted.

We set off for the picnic. Dora, her father, and
a friend, called Miss Mills, rode in an open carriage.
I rode behind it, looking at Dora.

There was a good deal of dust, I believe, from the
carriage wheels, but I saw and thought of nothing
but Dora.

I was sorry to find that other people had been invited to the party, because I wanted to have Dora to myself.

After dinner, Miss Mills, Dora, and I walked among the trees together. I kissed Dora's little hand, and she let me.

On the way home, Miss Mills whispered to me, 'Dora is coming to stay with me. If you would like to call, I'm sure my father would be glad to see you.'

How grateful I was to Miss Mills. I made up my mind to ask Dora to marry me the next time we met.

Three days later, I went to Miss Mills's house to see Dora.

I don't know how I did it, but I told Dora I loved her. I took her in my arms, and told her I should die without her. Jip barked madly all the time.

We became engaged, but kept our engagement a secret from Mr. Spenlow. Dora said that we were never to be married without her father's consent.

We met in secret and wrote letters every day, which Miss Mills agreed to deliver.

CHAPTER 20

Ruin

Peggotty and I came home one evening to find my aunt and Mr. Dick in my room. They were sitting on a pile of luggage.

'How glad I am to see you,' I cried.

'David, why do you think I am sitting on this luggage?' asked my aunt.

I could not guess.

'Because it is all I have,' she said. 'I am ruined. How can we live without money?'

I could hardly believe that she had lost all her money.

My aunt sent for Agnes Wickfield, and told her about her misfortune. Agnes told us that my old headmaster, Dr. Strong, was writing a dictionary, and needed a secretary.

'I'm sure he'd like to have you, David, better than anyone else,' said Agnes.

'Dear Agnes,' I said. 'What should I do without you? You are an angel.'

Dr. Strong had come to live in London. I went to see him, and he was delighted to employ me. I helped him in the early morning and in the evening after work.

Traddles found work for Mr. Dick to do, writing out copies of letters for lawyers.

'No starving now, David,' said Mr. Dick proudly, giving the ten shillings he had earned to my aunt.

Traddles brought me a letter from Mr. Micawber. He asked me to come and see him before he left London.

I went, and discovered that Mr. Micawber was going to Canterbury to become Uriah Heep's clerk. This was a great surprise to me.

95

When I told Dora that my aunt had lost her money, and that now I was a beggar, she shook her curls, and asked, 'How can you be such a silly thing?'

I begged her to learn to cook, and she began to cry. Still, I loved her as much as ever, and we wrote to one another every day.

When I told her I got up early to help Dr. Strong, she cried, 'It's so silly to get up early.'

'How can we live without working, Dora?'

'How? Anyhow!' said Dora.

96

One morning when I went to the office, I found
Mr. Spenlow looking very serious. He took me to a
coffee house where we met Miss Murdstone.

'Show Mr. Copperfield what you have in your
bag, Miss Murdstone,' he said.

She produced a packet of my letters to Dora.

'For some time I have thought Miss Spenlow was
getting too many letters from Miss Mills,' said Miss
Murdstone. 'Last night I saw Jip playing with
something. It was a letter from Mr. Copperfield,
which I read.'

'Have you anything to say?' asked Mr. Spenlow.

'Nothing, sir, except that the blame is mine, for keeping our engagement a secret.'

'Do not talk to me of engagements, Mr. Copperfield,' said Mr. Spenlow angrily, while Miss Murdstone laughed unpleasantly. 'I have other plans for my daughter's future. Put all thoughts of marrying her out of your mind, or I shall be forced to send her abroad.'

I was in despair. When I got home I told my aunt, but she could say nothing to comfort me.

Next day, when I went to the office, I found the clerks standing about, talking gravely.

'This is a dreadful misfortune, sir,' said one.

'What's the matter?' I asked.

'Mr. Spenlow—he's dead.'

'Dead?' said I.

'Last night he set off alone in his carriage, and he was found dead on the roadway, a mile from home.'

Dora was greatly upset by her father's death. She went to live with two unmarried aunts in Putney.

I asked Agnes Wickfield what I should do now.

'I think you ought to write to the two ladies, and tell them of your love for Dora,' she said. 'Ask them if you may visit them at their house.'

I sat down at once and wrote a letter to the Misses Spenlow.

CHAPTER 21

I Marry Dora

After a time the two old ladies invited me to visit them. Miss Lavinia and Miss Clarissa were Mr. Spenlow's sisters. They were dry little elderly ladies dressed in black.

'We have read your letter carefully, Mr. Copperfield,' said Miss Lavinia, 'and we have talked with our niece. We are sure you think you like her very much, but we must be sure you do. Therefore we shall allow you to visit us here.'

'I shall never forget your kindness,' I said.

'We shall be happy to see you to dinner every Sunday at three o'clock, and to tea twice a week at half past six,' said Miss Clarissa.

Miss Lavinia took me into another room. There I found Dora, hiding behind the door. How beautiful she was in her black frock. She sobbed and cried at first, and would not come out from behind the door. But when she did, how happy we were.

Only one thing troubled me. It was that everyone treated Dora like a toy. Even my aunt, when she met her, called her 'Little Blossom', and petted her.

After a time, Dora and I were married, and settled down in our own little house. I began to write books. Dora and Jip sat beside me as I worked in the evening.

Dora was not a good housekeeper. Our meals were often late, and badly cooked. If I spoke to her about it, she cried. When I learned not to expect too much from my child wife, we were very happy.

'I wish I could live for a year with Agnes,' said Dora. 'I think I could learn from her.'

At that time Agnes Wickfield had many worries of her own. Her father was ill, and the hateful Uriah Heep and his mother went to live in the Wickfield's house. Uriah wanted to marry Agnes, which made her friends very angry.

CHAPTER 22

Martha

One day as I passed Steerforth's house, a maid ran
out and said to me, 'Please come in and speak to
Miss Dartle.'

Rosa Dartle looked very grim, and asked, 'Has
the girl, Emily, been found?'

'No,' I replied.

'She has run away from Steerforth,' said Miss
Dartle. 'Steerforth's manservant told us they were
travelling abroad, and that they quarrelled in
Naples. Steerforth left her in charge of his servant,
who, he said, could marry her. Emily flew into a
rage and ran away.'

Mr. Peggotty was in London and I went at once to tell him that Emily was no longer with Steerforth.

'I think she will come and hide in London,' I said. 'I saw, one day, a poor girl whom Emily was kind to in Yarmouth. Martha is her name. Perhaps she could help us to look for Emily.'

'I know Martha,' said Mr. Peggotty.

We set off at once to find her. Suddenly we saw her hurrying along on the opposite pavement. She turned into a dark quiet road and we followed her as she went towards the river.

Martha seemed to be talking to herself as she hurried along. When she reached the river's edge, she looked as though she would throw herself in the water.

'Martha,' I said, grasping her arm.

She screamed with fright and almost fainted. Then she saw Mr. Peggotty whom she had known in Yarmouth, and she recovered a little. We carried her from the river, and talked to her. When she heard about Emily, she promised to do all she could to find her.

One evening, as I walked in my garden, someone called softly to me from the road. It was Martha.

'Can you come with me?' she said. 'I have been to see Mr. Peggotty, but he is not at home. I've left a letter for him.'

I followed Martha at once. We got into a coach, and drove to an old house in London. She led me to the top floor.

There was a bed in the bare attic, and Emily lay on the bed. Then we heard footsteps on the stairs, and Mr. Peggotty rushed past us into the room.

We heard Emily cry, 'Uncle!' and saw him lift her in his arms, and kiss her gently.

Mr. Peggotty took Emily to his lodgings, and they talked together the whole night through. He came to see me the next day, and told me that he and Emily were going to live far away, in Australia. Peggotty would stay behind in Yarmouth to look after Ham. He planned to leave Mrs. Gummidge enough money to live in the boat alone.

However, when Mrs. Gummidge heard that Mr. Peggotty was going to Australia, she begged to be taken too.

'Take me along with you and Em'ly,' she cried. 'I can work hard. I can be loving and patient. Let me go with you.'

Mr. Peggotty agreed to take her, and when they left Yarmouth together, Mrs. Gummidge looked happy at last.

CHAPTER 23

I Suffer Loss

Soon after Dora and I were married, she became ill.
She had to lie in bed all day, and my aunt helped
me to look after her.

'She will be better soon,' they told me, but instead, Dora became weaker and weaker.

'I want to see Agnes,' she said to me, one day. 'I
want to see her very much.'

I wrote to Agnes, and she came at once.

'Let me speak to Agnes alone,' said Dora.

I sat in the parlour with Jip, while Agnes went
upstairs to talk to Dora.

The little dog was restless. He stood at the door and whined to go upstairs. Then he came and licked my hand, and lay down at my feet. I thought he was asleep, but when I looked more closely, I saw he had died.

'Oh, Agnes, look! Look here!' I cried, when she came into the room.

Agnes was weeping. Her face was full of pity, for she had come to tell me that Dora was dead.

Both my aunt and Agnes were a great comfort to me in the sorrowful days that followed my wife's death. They decided that I should go abroad to recover from the shock.

Before I went, I paid a visit to Yarmouth to give Ham a farewell message from Emily. She was sailing to Australia with Mr. Peggotty and Mrs. Gummidge in a few days' time.

I travelled to Yarmouth on a stormy day. The wind blew hard. I spent the night at the inn, but could not sleep for the storm.

In the morning, someone knocked at my door and shouted:

'There's a wreck close by. Come quickly if you want to see her.'

I dressed and hurried out into the storm. There was the ship rolling on the huge waves. One mast was broken, and a torn sail flapped from the other. I could see a man with fair curling hair clinging to this mast.

The lifeboat had been launched but it could not reach the man in such a storm.

The wreck was slowly breaking to pieces.

Suddenly Ham appeared. He tied a rope round his waist, gave the end of it to his friends on the shore, and dashed into the sea.

He fought his way through the waves towards the wreck. Just when he came near it, a huge wave broke, and sank the ship.

The fishermen on shore pulled on the rope. They drew Ham's body from the water. He was dead.

As I sat beside Ham's body, a fisherman I knew came to me.

'Will you come, sir,' he said. 'Another body has been washed ashore.'

He led me to the spot where Mr. Peggotty's house had stood until last night, when the storm had blown it down.

There I saw Steerforth lying with his head upon his arm, as I had often seen him lie at school—but now he was dead. Ham had lost his life trying to save him from the wreck.

I had to go to Highgate to tell Mrs. Steerforth of her son's death. When I went into her room, the tears in my eyes alarmed her.

'My son is ill?' she said.

'Very ill.' I replied. 'There was a storm at sea——'

'Rosa, come to me,' said Mrs. Steerforth.

Rosa Dartle came. Her eyes were blazing with anger.

'Look at me,' she cried, striking the scar on her face. 'Do you remember when he did this? You spoiled him, but I loved him.' Then she turned to me and shouted, 'A curse upon you! Go!'

CHAPTER 24

The Emigrants

When I went to the ship to say good-bye to Mr.
Peggotty, Emily, and Mrs. Gummidge, I took care
not to tell them of the death of Ham and Steerforth.
I did not want to make them unhappy on their long
journey to Australia.

'Is there anything we have forgotten to say before
we part?' said Mr. Peggotty.

'One thing,' I said. 'Martha!'

He touched a young woman on the shoulder. She
turned, and I saw it was Martha. He was taking her
with them to Australia.

In the ship with them were Mr. and Mrs.
Micawber and their family. They, too, were going
to Australia to begin a new life.

When Mr. Micawber was working in Mr. Wickfield's office, he discovered that Uriah Heep was a
dishonest villain. He told Traddles and me of his
wickedness, and together we were able to turn
Uriah out of the business.

In the end, Uriah Heep was put into prison for
his dishonesty.

CHAPTER 25

I Return Home

I went to Switzerland, and stayed there for three years. I was sad and lonely after the death of my wife and my friends. I spent my time writing books, and I became well-known as an author.

Agnes wrote to me while I was abroad. She and her father were still living in the old house in Canterbury. They were happy now that they were free from Uriah Heep and his mother. Agnes was keeping a school for girls in their house. Her letters were a great comfort to me.

I wanted my return to London to be a surprise, so I told no one I was coming.

First, I went to see Traddles, at Gray's Inn. I heard laughter before I knocked at his door.

'My dearest Copperfield!' cried Traddles in surprise. 'How glad I am to see you. You might have come in time for the ceremony.'

'What ceremony, my dear Traddles?' I asked.

'My wedding. I am married. Look here.'

Sophy, the dearest girl in the world, came smiling from behind the curtains. I wished them both great joy.

Next, I went to see my aunt. She and Mr. Dick were living once more in the house at Dover, with Peggotty as their housekeeper. They greeted me with open arms and tears of joy.

My aunt and I sat very late, talking about the cheerful letters that had come from Australia. Mr. Micawber had even sent home small sums of money to pay his debts.

'And when are you going to Canterbury 'David?' asked my aunt, at last. 'Agnes has many admirers. I think she will marry soon.'

At Canterbury I found Agnes looking as beautiful and serene as ever. I went to visit her often during the next two months.

One day we sat talking on the window seat.

'Your writing has made you so famous,' she laughed, 'soon you won't want to talk to me.'

'All my life long I shall look up to you, and be guided by you, Agnes.' I said. 'You have always been like a sister to me. I shall always love you.'

As I watched Agnes sewing, I said to her:

'You have a secret. Let me share it, Agnes. Tell me who it is you are going to marry. I promise I shall not be jealous.'

Agnes rose, put her hands over her face and burst into tears.

'Agnes, dearest, what have I said? If you are unhappy, let me share your unhappiness.'

'My secret is an old one, which I cannot share with anyone,' said Agnes. 'Let me go away, David. I am not well. Don't speak to me now.'

I took Agnes in my arms and said to her:

'I went away, dear Agnes, loving you. I stayed away, loving you. I returned home loving you. When I lost Dora, what should I have been without you?'

Agnes was still weeping, but joyfully—not sadly,

'There is one thing I must say to you,' she said. laying her gentle hands on my shoulders.

'Tell me, my dear.'

'I have loved you all my life,' she said.

Next day I took Agnes to visit my aunt. Miss Betsey sat by the fire as darkness was falling.

'Who is this you are bringing home?' she asked.

'Agnes,' I said.

We both leaned over her chair. She took one look at us through her spectacles, and for the first time of her life she had hysterics.

She hugged Peggotty who hurried in to see what was the matter. Then she hugged Mr. Dick who looked surprised. When she told them we were to be married, we were all very happy together.

Agnes and I were married within a fortnight. As we drove away from the church together, Agnes said to me:

'Dearest husband, I have one more thing to tell you.'

'Let me hear it, my love.'

'The night she died, Dora made one last request to me,' said Agnes.

'And it was——?' I asked.

'That only I should fill this vacant place,' she replied.

I drew her closer to me, and we wept together, though we were so happy.

Notes

CHAPTER I
a parlour: a sitting-room.
a bonnet: a hat tied on with strings or ribbons.

CHAPTER 2
a workbox: a box for holding sewing materials.
handsome: good looking.
whiskers: hair on the cheeks.
a fortnight: two weeks.
a carrier: a person who takes goods from one place to another.
canvas: strong, coarse cloth.

CHAPTER 3
a looking-glass: a mirror.
snug: comfortable, cosy.
brother-in-law: the husband of Mr. Peggotty's sister.
'I'm a lone lorn creature': 'I'm a lonely, miserable person.'
contrary: wrong.

CHAPTER 4
to fuss: to bustle about; to worry.
harsh: severe; unkind.
a household: the people in a house.
a cane: a stick.
a keyhole: a hole in the door made for the key.

CHAPTER 5
to protect: to defend.
to introduce: to make one person known to another.

CHAPTER 6
gruffly: roughly.
glancing: looking at.
delicate: frail; not strong.
to disturb: to trouble; to break the rest of someone.

CHAPTER 7

a study: a room to study in.
a couch: a settee.
a funeral: the burying of someone who is dead.

CHAPTER 8

a wine merchant: someone who sells wine.
a cellar: a place below the ground for storing wine.
to lodge: to stay in rooms in someone else's house.
shabby: old, worn out.
a commercial traveller: someone who travels about to get orders for his firm.
credit: time to pay accounts.
a tradesman: a shopkeeper, or a skilled worker.
a prison: a place where people who have broken the law are locked up.
debt: money owed to someone.

a coach: a large closed carriage with seats inside, and on the roof for passengers. People travelled by coach before trains and buses were invented.

CHAPTER 9

belongings: possessions; things that belong to you.
to plod: to walk on and on.
half-naked: almost without clothes.
ragged: in rags.

CHAPTER 10

a nephew: the son of a brother or sister.
a kite: a frame covered with paper that flies in the wind.
to ill-treat: to be cruel; to treat badly.
to befriend: to be kind; to help.

NOTES

CHAPTER 11

a lawyer: a person who has studied law.

'umble: humble; modest; meek.

I had no business to tell: I ought not to have told.

in the hope that something would turn up: hoping that something good would happen to him.

CHAPTER 12

information: knowledge.

a scar: a mark left after a wound has healed.

an inn: an hotel.

rheumatic: suffering from pains in the joints.

a tassel on his nightcap:

the master of a boat: the captain.

CHAPTER 13

an apprentice: someone who is learning a job.

the firm: the business.

a landlady: a person who keeps a boarding-house, or lodgings.

a pantry: a store room.

CHAPTER 14

a partner: a person who shares in a business with others.

to dine: to have dinner.

CHAPTER 15

a carriage: in the old days, people used a carriage as we use a motor-car.

a companion: someone who is paid to live with another person.

you have your opinion of me: you know what you think of me.

to gaze: to look steadily at.

to thrill: to delight.

to snarl: to growl.

fancy waistcoats: embroidered or coloured waistcoats.

CHAPTER 16

a curate: a clergymen; a minister.

to become engaged: to agree to marry someone.

to board with someone: to pay for rooms in their house.

127

NOTES

CHAPTER 17

a will: written instructions about what is to be done with our belongings when we die.

a sou'wester: a waterproof hat.

CHAPTER 18

a career: a way of making a living.

oilskin: waterproof.

CHAPTER 20

a dictionary: a book which tells the meanings of words.

a secretary: someone who helps with letters and written work.

a beggar: a very poor person; one who begs.

a coffee house: a shop where coffee and refreshments are served.

gravely: seriously.

CHAPTER 21

Little Blossom: Little Flower.

CHAPTER 22

grim: severe, hard.

attic: a room on the top floor of a house.

CHAPTER 23

to whine: to cry, as a dog cries.

to weep: to cry.

a wreck: a damaged ship.

to alarm: to frighten.

CHAPTER 24

an emigrant: someone who leaves one country to settle in another.

CHAPTER 25

serene: calm.

famous: well known.

jealous: envious.

hysterics: a fit of laughing and crying.

to make a request: to ask someone to do something.

vacant: empty.

Uriah Heep

Ham

Betsey Trotwood

Dora

David

Peggotty

Barkis

Miss Murdstone

Traddles

Mr. Dick

Emily

Steerforth

Mr. Peggotty

Agnes

Mr. Micawber

Mrs. Steerforth

Mr. Murdstone

Rosa Dartle